Challenge of Culture in Africa

Challenge of Culture in Africa

From Restoration to Integration

Bernard N. Fonlon

Langaa Research & Publishing CIG
Mankon, Bamenda

Publisher:
Langaa RPCIG
Langaa Research & Publishing Common Initiative Group
P.O. Box 902 Mankon
Bamenda
North West Region
Cameroon
Langaagrp@gmail.com
www.langaa-rpcig.net

Distributed outside N. America by African Books
Collective
orders@africanbookscollective.com
www.africanbookscollective.com

Distributed in N. America by Michigan State
University Press
msupress@msu.edu
www.msupress.msu.edu

ISBN: 9956-578-98-3

DISCLAIMER

The names, characters, places and incidents in this book are either the product of the author's imagination or are used fictitiously. Accordingly, any resemblance to actual persons, living or dead, events, or locales is entirely one of incredible coincidence.

Contents

Audendo atque **agendo** res Romana crevit, non his segnibus conciliis quac timidi cauta vocant (Anon)

It was by **daring** and by **doing** that the Roman state grew, and not by the timid policies that cowards call caution.

Part One
Culture as Tillage

In a treatise of this nature one forestalls confusion and misunderstanding and irrelevant wrangling by defining one's terms. Therefore, concerning **Cultural Integration in Cameroon**, it will serve a useful purpose, if I say precisely what I mean by culture, what I mean by integration, what I mean by Cameroon.

The present essay will deal entirely with the first of these terms.

In the Latin of Vergil, Horace and Livy there was a verb **colo, colere, colui, cultum**, to till. Its corresponding noun was **cultura**, tilling, tillage.

By the Middle Ages, the classical colo had been corrupted into **cultivo, cultivare, cultivatum**, with **cultivatio** for its noun. Thus **culture** and **cultivation** are very close synonyms.

According to its root, therefore, the word culture belongs to the farm. For vegetal growth to be possible, as we are told in elementary nature study, there must be, on the one hand, the seed with the tree and the harvest sleeping within it; there must be, on the other, the elements: soil, water, air, heat and light. When seeds fall at random in the jungle where the elements are gracious, there will be growth. But this growth will be haphazard, unaided, impeded. As a result, the issuing plants will be wild in their state, disorderly in their disposition, stunted or diminutive in size and poor in their quality and yield.

Furthermore, husbandry, as we know, includes the rearing not only of plants but also of animals. And where the skill of the husbandman has not been brought to bear, wildness in the beast can mean not only disorder but also violence and danger.

3

Tillage means the intervention of man, the intervention of intelligence, in the growth of plants.

Thanks to his reason, man brings far reaching influences to bear in the growth of vegetation. These are purpose, knowledge, energy and skill.

Driven by a **need,** the need to satisfy his hunger, man realises that this hunger will best be allayed if the food-producing plant is enabled to attain the fullness of its being and yield its richest. His **purpose** therefore is two-fold-a proximate and an ultimate: proximately he intends to produce the most perfect plant of the kind, and ultimately to allay his hunger with the fruits thereof, and thus enjoy a measure of satisfaction or happiness.

Through previous observation and reflection, man, in embarking on tillage, is equipped with **knowledge:** knowledge of the nature and of the needs of plants, knowledge of the nature of the elements and of the conditions and the operations necessary for earth and water and air and sun to further luxuriant growth.

Furthermore, the surface of the soil is encumbered by masses of un-wanted vegetation that must be forced to give way, and sometimes even by stumps and rocks and stones that must be dug up and removed; plant food is buried deep and must be put within easy reach of roots. All this clearing and delving entails arduous **labour.**

But labour alone however strenuous will not do; it must be labour guided by knowledge; it must be the faithful translation into practice, by the hand, of the theories thought out, by the head, on how to foster the growth of plants. It must be labour plus **skill.**

Thanks to tillage, therefore, thanks to the purpose, the knowledge, the labour and the skill of man, that which would have been wild becomes **tame,** that which would have been scattered at haphazard is set **in order,** that which would

4

have been stunted attains its **plenitude** and a yield that would have been lean becomes **rich** both in quality and in quantity.

But the question still remains: what is tillage in itself, what is its nature?

In the first place, tillage begins as **action,** namely, the operation of cultivating land to fit it for crops; the tending of the crops planted on land thus prepared. And, considered as action, tillage points to a tiller.

Secondly, this action produces a **state** in that which is tilled: the soil is rid of the rough and harmful and rendered more fertile, the crops are arranged in orderly fashion; the state where that which should not be is removed, where that which should be is set in order, rendered better: the state of being tame-cultivated.

Thirdly, the word culture is applied to the final **product** that results from the operation and the state of cultivation, namely the crops growing on tilled land, the harvest therefrom.

Action, state, and result are intrinsically linked together, are but stages in one and the same process.

Let it be noted however that the action and the state are transient whereas the result is permanent; the action and the state are means whereas the produce is the end. More, not only is the harvest the more permanent stage, the end and purpose of the whole operation, it is also the guarantee for continuity since the harvest is not only food but also seed.

To sum up: four forces or causes concur in tillage. First, the tiller, equipped within and without – without with tools, within with skill and knowledge: he is the efficient cause of tillage. Next comes the purpose that spurs the delver on, namely, the absolute need to satisfy his hunger and attain thereby a certain measure of happiness: this is the ultimate end or the final cause of his endeavours. Third, there is the concrete thing that the tiller strives to bring into being by all his labours: naturally, every tiller toils and moils to produce the most perfect plant of the kind, the most verdant and exuberant field, the richest harvest possible: this is the formal cause of tillage. Finally, there are the various elements which combine to make up the physical substance itself of the perfect plant, namely the seed, on the one hand, and soil, water, air, heat and light, on the other: these constitute the material cause of tillage.

These forces, therefore, exerting themselves in concert, set the process of tillage in motion; and, in this progress, as we have -seen, there are four stages: the **action** of the tiller, the **state** that this action produces in land and crops, the more luxuriant **growth** that this action and state stimulate in plants and the richer **harvest** that these yield, thanks to action, state and growth. These stages are so necessarily linked together that when we talk of tillage, in the fullest sense of the term, we include all of them at least implicitly; in other words, although this process proceeds by stages clear and distinct, it is one and indivisible, it is held together by ties of intrinsic necessity.

From all that has gone before, tillage can therefore be defined as bringing the growth of plants under the control of right reason, guiding the growth of plants according to sound knowledge and skill in order to enable them to attain the fullness of their being and yield their richest and best.

I said at the start that, according to its etymology, the word culture belongs to the farm and means the tilling or **the cultivation of land**. In this particular sense, however, it has been made more specific by the prefix **agri**- (from the Latin **agrum, agri**, a field): agriculture.

The root word culture, thanks to analogy, is now reserved for a higher kind of tillage: today, when we use the word culture we mean almost exclusively **the cultivation of man**.

Yet, culture thus understood, remains real tillage, notwithstanding.

For there, the four causes operative in tillage are all present: there are soil and seed, there is a tiller, there is a purpose and there is perfection of being to be achieved. Present too are the four stages of the tillage process: there is action, there is a state induced, there is growth and there is a harvest.

Man as an **individual** and as **society**, man with his physical and spiritual faculties-his senses, his mind, his feelings and his will-is the soil; knowledge and skill and virtue are the seed.

Man is the tiller. And here is a thing worthy of note, that, in this higher tillage, man is tiller and tilled both in one. He is both, first in the strict sense that each human being cultivates himself, cultivates his faculties, takes an active and essential part in his own education; man is tiller and tilled in the wider social sense that some human beings cultivate others, the generation that goes before educates that which follows after.

There is an ultimate purpose for the tillage of man: just as the final end of ordinary agriculture is to obtain for man a degree of **happiness** by satisfying his physical hunger, just so the ultimate intention of culture is to procure for him happiness of a higher nature, first by a thorough, deep and balanced development of his faculties, that is, his senses, his feeling, his mind and his will, and next by supplying each faculty with the nourishment for which it hungers: truth for the mind, goodness for the will and beauty for sense and feeling.

Finally, just as tillers of the soil aim at producing the **perfect plant**, in like manner tillers of men aim at rearing the **perfect human being**. Thus every society, every system of philosophy that has ever preoccupied itself with the rearing of children has always defined, explicitly or impli-citly, its idea of the perfect man, its ideal man.

Furthermore, as we have seen, in the cultural process, the four stages that we saw in tillage are clearly evident: action, state, growth and fruit.

Action in the tilling of men deserves special note because, unlike its counterpart in the tilling of land where it is exerted almost exclusi-vely by the tiller alone, active effort here is demanded from both the tiller and the tilled; for in fact, as education progresses, an increasingly greater exertion is required from the learner than from the teacher: far from being passive, learning is essentially an active process. More-over, when you consider the fact, that human nature is corrupt and more powerfully inclined to evil than to good, to ease than to toil; when you consider how much repetition, how many years of ceaseless drudgery are required before sense and mind and will and feeling are trained to an appreciable degree, before any standard of education worthwhile is reached, you see clearly that the cultivation of man is, in its very nature, an extremely difficult operation.

The labours of teacher and learner sharpen the senses, rid the mind of error and sow knowledge, bend the will to seek good and shun evil, to love the right and hate the wrong, and train the feelings to find their joy in that which is truly beautiful. In this fashion, these labours eliminate what should not be, foster what should, and produce order and harmony and balance in man, and thus, induce the state of cultivation, of refinement.

Evidently, cultural action promotes growth, the child's senses become keener, his mind develops, his skill becomes more perfect, his knowledge increases, his will grows firmer in the right.

There is growth also for society; for, each generation, using the cultural legacy that it has inherited from the past, enriches this legacy further with new discoveries of its own in science and philosophy, new creations in art; and, thus, the sum of human culture grows from more to more, grows better and better, as ages course along.

Just as in tillage, culture as action and state is transient: the tiller rests, his toiling over; the field lapses into fallow; generations pass; but the harvest of culture remains and guarantees continuity. That is why, when we talk of culture, we are naturally inclined to think less of the process of education and human refinement, but more of the rich and varied content of civilization – of the arts and the sciences, of ethics and mores, of social institutions, of systems of abstract thought.

Just like unaided seed, children on whom no care is lavished, can grow somehow or other. Imaginative writers tell us of cases where children have survived in the most unbelievable conditions; Tennyson in one of his poems mentions the case of the Britain of long ago and its

> ... great tracts of wilderness
> Wherein the beast was ever more and more
>
> But man was less and less, till Arthur came...
> And ever and anon the wolf...,
> Her own brood lost or dead, lent her fierce teat
> to human sucklings; and the children, housed
> In her foul den, there at their meal would growl,
> And mock their foster mother on four feet,
> Till straightened, they grew up into wolf-like men,
> Worse than the wolves.[1]

Whether what the poet recounts be true or merely a fiction of a fertile imagination, this much, at least, is beyond dispute: human nature left alone is more inclined to waywardness and indocility than to virtue and knowledge and, therefore, if children are left without proper and adequate tending, they will grow up nearer to the wolf than to man, lawless, wild, dark in mind; and, their moral and mental development thus arrested for ever, they will be rendered, in life, completely incapable of any achievement worthy of man.

Culture can, therefore, be succinctly defined as bringing the growth of man under the control of right reason, guiding the growth of man according .to sound knowledge, in order to enable him to attain perfect being, perfect manhood, so that his genius may flower and yield undying fruit in the shape of profound and deathless doctrine, heroic moral example, scientific discoveries, artistic masterpieces.

The Genesis of Culture

Culture has a two-fold origin, a psychological and a historical, that is, culture takes birth in man, and at a point of time, in the story of the world. I do not intend here to go into the origin and the evolution of culture through the ages. My intention is to find out how culture is born in man so that, from his investigation, I may acquire a clearer and deeper understanding of its nature.

Culture takes rise from this that man is born into the world incomplete. Not that at birth he lacks any part necessary to make him a full human being, but that, although complete with regard to his composition, he is still incomplete with regard to his physical extension; incomplete in this that his spiritual faculties, though really present, are still lying dormant awaiting time and exercise and growth to attain maturity.

Furthermore, to make life easier for animals, nature not only supplies them with some of their needs directly (coats of hair for animals, and feathers for birds) but endows others with complete skills which they ply without any previous apprenticeship whatsoever-witness the bee, witness the ant, witness the nest-building birds.

On the contrary, man is not born innately supplied with knowledge and skill. He is equipped with reason and left to fend for himself, to use his mind to solve for himself the problems of his existence.

Briefly, therefore, man is not born in the fullness of his being; and thus in order to survive, to live and develop in himself, he has **need** of many things external to himself.

Furthermore, even when he has attained the flower of his manhood, other needs still remain; for, from the cradle to the grave, man is racked by a hundred undying thirsts; he is like a void that never fills. In other words, man has various needs of a **permanent** nature.

Since these needs are ever-present, ever-gnawing, it is necessary for man to forge permanent ways of satisfying them. It is in the search for ways and means to supply his wants that man creates culture.

The psychological origin of any given cultural element, therefore, is a specific human need.

Each human need poses a problem. To solve this problem man has to **think**. He has to think because he is surrounded by a hundred things and he has to know both the nature of his need and the nature of things to determine which of them can satisfy that need. Furthermore, there are few cases, like that of water and thirst, for example, where the thing as it is can directly supply the need.

But more often than not, the thing has to be transformed in order to suit his need: food must be cultivated and prepared, shelter and clothing must be fashioned from suitable material. Through observation thought and experiment, man finally discovers or elaborates a method of carrying out such a transformation, and through more observation, more thought and more experiment improves upon this method.

As we all know, man can satisfy his needs only by using the things that surround him in the external world, and to fit thing to need he must think. But he cannot think about the world outside his mind unless that outside world is somehow or other represented in his mind. **Happily**, thanks to his senses and to abstraction, man is able to create in his mind ideas on concepts of the things about him. Therefore, for every object that exists, there is a corresponding concept. And it is by comparing concepts to see the relations they bear one to the other that man thinks.

But in order to render these concepts more precise, in order to be able to state more clearly, even to himself, the problems he encounters and the solutions he forges for them, in order to communicate these answers to others, in order to preserve them for posterity, man needs something in addition to concepts, namely, a means of expressing these concepts verbally, externally. He needs to give names to things and to the relations that exist between them; in short, he needs language.

There are three things, therefore, in this process: **the world of things** gives rise to **the world of thought** and the world of thought engenders **the world of verbal expression**.

Next to thought, **language is the first cultural necessity, the first cultural invention of man. There can be no culture without language, no language without culture. Culture and language, or expression, are one.**

If a given substance is to be transformed into a definite state each time the process is performed, that process of transformation must be consistent and constant. In other words, there is no method where things are done at haphazard; for method, there must be logical thought, there must be a system.

Each cultural element, each thought-out method of supplying a human need is such a system.

A system exists where there are parts which not only hold together to form one whole, but operate together, one depending on the other and on the whole. Thanks to thought, each such system possesses a rigorous logical order within itself, the logical order that exists between cause and effect.

In other words, any given cultural element is something organised, that is, something composed of well-related organs.

The word **organum**, from which organ comes, originally meant an instrument, or more precisely, a musical instrument; and we know that harmony is produced when many musical instruments so blend with each other as to produce one symphony. We also know that the skill of the virtuoso awakens the instrument out of silence and gives it piercing expression, makes it alive, as it were. Today, moreover, when we hear the word organ, we are immediately reminded of a living body; for an organ thus understood is a part or a member of an animal or plant body adapted by its structure to a particular vital function-the eye for seeing, for instance. And thus an organic structure or an organism is a body composed of organs, **endowed with life**.

In like manner culture is organised, organic, also in the sense that it is something living – the permanent stimulus and guide in human action.

Thus, any given cultural element is something organised not merely in the sense that it is a system endowed with internal logic or order but also because it is an organ in the life of man. For there are two things in human life, first his being or his **esse** and then his activity or his **agere**. If the esse is living, the **agere** also must be living.

And culture is the driving force in man's rational activity; for if activity is to be rational it must be governed by principle, and we get our principles of life from our culture.

Therefore and above all, culture is something living because it is essentially thought and thought is the principal act of conscious being. Culture is essentially thought because however concrete, however complicated. a thing created may be, man, before realising that creation, must think it out thoroughly and completely; and the act of realising it in the concrete must be guided, all along, by the mental expression that man first formulates of that creation in the mind.

All culture therefore is, first and essentially, thought or organic expression.

We can sum up then by saying that, at the bottom of any given cul-tural element, there is a burning human need. Driven by this need, and helped by observation and experiment, the human mind-the supreme architect of culture-elaborates a system of thought laying down a method of using the external world to satisfy that need.

And since human life is one, since the members of the human person are interdependent, since the various levels of human life are inextricably linked one with the other, human needs are therefore inter-related, and, consequently, the various cultural elements forged by man to satisfy his needs must be interdependent too.

Thus the corpus of all the systems elaborated by any particular human group to allay its needs constitutes an organic cultural whole.

There is no people so god-forsaken, so backward, but must have its own culture, its own answers to the eternal problems of life.

And since human nature is one, and since the problems that beset man are the same all over, there must be something common to all cultures at all places and at all times. Thus no culture is completely foreign. It is this communion of nature and of need that makes cultural borrowing possible.

And yet cultures differ considerably one from the other. This is so because some regions and ages have stimulated human endeavour more than others. Some peoples, now and again, have been favoured more than others with minds fertile and effective above the ordinary.

For, in cultural progress, it is astounding to see how much the world owes to the isolated genius of individuals, men who saw far ahead of their times, men with revolutionary ideas. Think of Aristotle, think of Christ, think of the modern conquerors of space.

In the cultural field, indeed, the saying that one man can change the world is literally true.

But where nature has been gracious, where the sting of want has. been less piercing, where people have sunk back into complacent certi-tude, untroubled by doubt and numb to the spirit that urges inquiry, minds have remained beclouded, and cultural output unimpressive.

The Purpose of Culture

As we, have seen above, culture, considered as action produced by a subject on an object, is the cultivation of man.

The first endowment that a human person gets on coming into the universe is to exist, **being**, that is. But this being, as we all know, is incomplete with regard to its physical extension and dormant with regard to its spiritual powers. Thus, if this being has to realise its fullest self, it must possess an additional power – the power of **becoming**, in other words, the power to develop. From the moment of his conception the human being strains towards this fullness of development; and there can be no complete well-being until man completely becomes what he ought to be.

To attain this plenitude, as we. have seen, man must be forever striving to supply many an ever-gnawing need. For this, he must exercise his mind to elaborate permanent solutions to all these problems of sense, feeling, mind and will. This very exercise is an indispensable factor in the furthering of mental growth; for, as any other faculty, the mind develops by exerting itself.

The solution of the problems posed by needs involves two things: the clearing away of obstacles and injurious things, on the one hand, the attainment and enjoyment of that which is craved for, on the other; **aliis verbis**, the elimination of evil and the joyful possession of good. When all evil is removed and all the good necessary is put there to be enjoyed, there is satisfaction, in other words, there is happiness.

And happiness is the highest good of man, the final purpose of all human striving.

Cicero defines it as:

Secretis malis omnibus cumulata bonorum omnium complexio:
The sum total of all that is good when all that is evil has been removed[2].

Another ancient writer, Boethius, says that it is:

Status omnium bonorum congregatione perjectus:
The perfect state attained by the accumulation of all good[3].

St. Thomas Aquinas calls it:

Bonum perfectum intellectualis naturae:
The perfect good of a nature with a mind[4].

And the Roman satirist, Juvenal, after demonstrating the vanity of human wishes asserts that the highest object of human prayer should be:

Ut sit mens sana in corpore sano:
For a sound mind in a sound body[5].

It is, therefore, in the satisfaction of his needs, in the full and harmonious development of body, sense, feeling, mind and will, in the acquisition of physical vigour, knowledge, virtue, creative imagination, artistic skill, **it is in the attainment of perfection, that man can find genuine happiness**. And all this cannot be achieved without cultivation, without culture.

We can therefore say that **the purpose of culture is to help man to achieve the fullness of his being and thereby to attain real happiness**.

The African Ideal

As I have said before, culture, considered as the cultivation of man, is synonymous with education. Wherever there are human beings in need of growth, wherever there are children to be brought up, there must be some system of education.

The nature of this system of education will depend, in the main on what sort of individual that particular society wants to produce, on what is their idea of the perfect man. And their idea of the perfect man will depend, to a large extent, on the problems that beset that society; for their ideal man will be the man best equipped, best able to meet these problems. Was there then a system of education for African children before the white man came?

Unquestionably!

What then was the African idea of the perfect man?

There are still among us, today, those who saw the initiation system.

And from the tests in hardihood that it involved, we can assert with certainty that **the aim of the African system for the upbringing of children was the production of a man, the individual endowed with manliness, with virility**. The aim of that education was to harden, to instil discipline, fearlessness, endurance'. The African system of education was steeped in the ancient conviction that fighting is the only noble thing.

> **The principle it strove to instil was that a man should rather die than surrender his manhood**.

In the history of early European education, a distinction was made between the education of the scribe and the education of the warrior, of the hero. In pre-colonial days the scribe had not yet made his appearance on the African scene and so our ancestors gave all their attention to rearing of the warrior.

The word education is derived from the Latin verb **educo, educare, educatum**, to rear, to bring up, that is, a child.

Education has been aptly and comprehensively defined as the phy-sical, the aesthetic, the intellectual and the moral up-bringing of man.

This definition is based on, and is justified by, the fact that man has a body, senses internal and external, a mind and a will to drill and to train up from an infant stage to maturity. And since a full human life is impossible, if any of these is missing, an ideal education, there-fore, consists in the complete and balanced development of all of them together.

Each of these faculties is trained by two essential exercises: first by furnishing it with the object for which it was made, the object for which it yearns like we do for food and drink; secondly, by making it use the energy obtained from this nourishment to acquire more of what it needs, by making it use this energy also (especially when It takes the form of intellectual attainment) to solve the problems of human life and win, thereby, more happiness for the individual and for the community.

Thus, for example, by wholesome food and arduous outdoor exercise, a person develops a sturdy muscular frame, becomes steeled in manly hardihood, stores up funds of physical energy and becomes, thereby, capable of increased bodily exertion, of more needful toil. This is the physical side of education – an essential one.

In like manner, the senses, through contact with the external world, can be drilled to dwell upon and appreciate the multiform beauty that exists in colour, shape, sound and action, so that man, by means of fertile imagination and penetrating intelligence, can use the images, memories and reflections garnered from this contemplation and meditation to create masterpieces in painting, sculpture, architecture, music and literature. This is the aesthetic side of education – a highly useful one.

In the same way, the mind, through observation, learning and study is fed with knowledge and is charged with vigorous health especially where this mental nourishment, this knowledge, is not only wholesome and abundant but also organised. For a head with order inside it is far better than one that is full but confused. By enquiry, experiment and reflection, knowledge grows deeper, wider, richer; the mind's scope tor more becomes larger, its power for long retention grows stronger, and its skill for getting at the truth is rendered surer. This is the intellectual side of education – a clearly obvious one, in fact so obvious that men have almost come to regard it as the only one. The supreme importance of this aspect of education, therefore, cannot become the subject of debate; for it is intellectual training that enables man to use, not only knowledge but also physical endowment and attainment, artistic skill and moral principle to solve the problems of life or to win more happiness for the individual and the community, or, indeed, for the human race as a whole.

Furthermore, human passions are so restive, so difficult to curb, so prone to carry us astray that the effort to live aright becomes a relentless, life-long warfare. Yet, by constancy and firmness in choosing good and rejecting evil, in doing the right and shunning the wrong, man can render his will ever stronger and can, thereby, rise, step by step, from the levels of ordinary goodness up the heights of heroic virtue. This is the moral aspect of education-an absolutely indispensable one.

As I have said above, the intensive exercise of any of the faculties on its formal object keeps the level of its receptive capacity and the degree of its active efficiency on the rise; furthermore, if this intensive training is fostered early and pursued unswervingly for an adequate length of time, the powers of the faculty remain active far into declining years.

Such is education rightly and comprehensively understood.

The ancients were therefore wrong in dividing men into heroes and scribes and prescribing a special and exclusive type of education for each group. For, as we have seen, a genuine system of education should strive to make man scholar and hero both in one, because, as I have shown, the ideal man, the perfect man, is he in whom physical, aesthetic, intellectual and moral faculty and attainment are developed to the utmost.

But, in the raising of their sons, our ancestors, partly because their knowledge of the nature of things was rudimentary and stagnant, partly because of the bristling foes that harried them without respite on every side, concentrated all but the whole of their attention on instilling manly courage, on arousing martial daring.

The African ideal of the perfect man therefore was the virile man.

But we must make it clear that the African principle that the purpose of education is to teach men to fight did not limit this warfare to physical combat only. We are told that in the initiation ceremonies young men were specially put to the test to find out, for instance, whether they could resist sexual lust. For, in the African mind, evil and vice are as much an enemy as an armed foe on the field of battle.

In the African way of thinking, the virile man had also to be a virtuous man, a man engaged in war against all that **his society believed** to be wrong.

Educating to Unman

W hen colonialism came, it realised naturally that this warrior spirit was its most dangerous enemy. Colonialism cannot thrive where there is no submission. And if there is to be submission, the colonised must be disarmed in body and soul, their spirit must be broken, the warrior must be reduced into a cringing coward.

And thus wherever you find it, from ancient days to ours, colonialism has always aimed at stripping men of their manhood –at total emasculation.

This it achieves in two ways. The first and obvious one is by striking terror into its victims by the use of might. That is why it is rare in history to find any colonial subjugation that was not accompanied by brute force.

Of all the literature I have read on colonialism I have nowhere found a description that hits that system off so tersely and so tellingly as a passage in a. speech that Tacitus, the Roman historian, in his life of Agricola, his father-in-law and Roman Governor in Britain, reports to have been made by a British chief, Calgacus by name, haranguing his hordes before joining battle, when the Briton rose, in 83 A.D. to strike for the Island's freedom against the might and rule of Rome.

Talking about Roman imperialism the Briton said:

Auferre, trucidare, rapere,
falsis nominibus imperium
atque ubi solitudinem faciunt,
pacem appellant[6].

Robbery, butchery and rapine
the liars call empire;
and when they make a desert,
they call it peace.

In fact, in all colonial history we read of pacification; and this has always meant the same thing: the use of armed might to reduce its victims to silence, the silence of the wilderness, the silence of fear.

The second effective way whereby colonial rulers unman their victims is through education.

Under colonial government the new education is reserved for the few; and to these few it is not manly courage and valour that are held up as ideals worthy of their pursuit. No, rather it is pleasure; it is the hoarding of wealth, of money, as the surest road to pleasure. And colonial conquerors have always known that **there is hardly a means more insidious, more infallible of emptying a people of manliness and making them willing slaves than to excite, especially in their elite and leadership, an insatiable thirst for pleasure**. Soon the spirit gets esta-blished that pleasure is the highest good and a deadly germ of ruin sets to work within the very vitals of that society. Hedonism, as this philosophy is called, is, indeed, one of the archenemies of human freedom. This colonial education policy was no brain wave hit upon in recent times by the genius of any empire-building schemer in London or Paris. The Romans knew it long ago.

For, writing about the education policy of the same Roman Governor, Agricola, for his British subjects, Tacitus has this to report:

Namque ut homines dispersi ac rudes eoque in bella faciles quieti et otio per voluptates adsuescerent, hortari privatim, adiuvare publice,

ut templa fora domos extruerent, laudando
promptos et castigando segnes : ita honoris
aemulatio pro necessitate erat.

lam vero principum filios liberalibus artibus
erudire, et ingenia Britannorum studiis Gallorum
anteierre, ut qui modo linguam Romanam
abnuebant, eloquentiam concupiscerent. Inde
etiam habitus nostri honor et jrequens toga.
Paulatimque discessum ad delenimenta vitiorum,
porticus et balinea et conviviorum elegantiam:
Idque apud imperitos humanitas vocabatur, cum
pars servitutis esset[7].

In order that a people scattered and uncivilized, and for
that reason ever ready to fight, should be accustomed
through lives of pleasure to peace and tranquillity, he
encouraged them privately and assisted them publicly, in
erecting temples, market-places, and houses, praising the
forward and censuring the slothful, so that rivalry for honour
took the place of compulsion.

Then he began to give the sons of chiefs a liberal
education and was wont to express a preference for the
natural talents of the Britons as against the industry of the
Gauls, with the result that a nation which had lately rejected
the Roman language were now eager to learn eloquence.
Next even our manner of dress became a distinction, and
the toga was frequently to be seen. Gradually they turned
aside to the things which make vice seductive, porticoes,
baths, and luxurious banquets. And this, in their simple-
mindedness, they called civilization whereas it was only
another means of their enslavement.

Clear-sighted fighters for freedom have always been quick
to see the perniciousness of colonial education; and, more
often than not, they have singled it out as the object of
special wrath.

Padraic Pearse, the famous Irish revolutionary, spoke with extreme violence against the system of education set up by the British in Ireland. **He** called it **The Murder Machine:** a soulless thing which far from teaching destroys; a machine which cannot make men, but can break them.

I have spent (he said) the greater part of my life in immediate contemplation of the most grotesque and horrible of the English inventions for the debasement of Ireland. I mean their education system. The English once proposed in their Dublin Parliament a measure for the castration of all Irish priests who refused to quit Ireland. The proposal was so filthy that, although it duly passed the House and was transmitted to England with the warm recommen-dation of the Viceroy, it was not eventually adopted. But the English have actually carried out an even filthier thing. They have planned and established an education system which more wickedly does violence to the elementary human rights of Irish children than would an edict for the general castration of Irish males. The system has aimed at the substitution for men and wonum of mere Things. It has not been an entire success. There are still a great many thousand men and women in Ireland. But a great many thousand of what, by way of courtesy, we call men and women, are simply Things. Men and women, however depraved, have kindly human allegiances. But these Things have no allegiance. Like other Things, they are for sale.

The English have established the simulacrum of an education system, but its object is the precise contrary of the object of an education system. Education should foster; this education is meant to repress. Education should inspire; this education is meant to tame. Education should harden,' this education is meant to enervate. The English are too wise a people to attempt to educate the Irish, in any worthy sense. As well expect them to arm us ...

I would urge that the Irish school system of the future should give freedom-freedom to the individual school, freedom to the individual teacher, freedom as far as may be to the individual pupil. Without freedom there can be no right growth; and education is properly the fostering of the right growth of a personality. Our school system must bring, too, some gallant inspiration. And with the inspiration it must bring a certain hardening. One scarcely knows whether modern sentimentalism or modern utilitarianism is the more sure sign of modern decadence. I would boldly preach the antique faith that fighting is the only noble thing, and that he only is at peace with God who is at war with the powers of evil...

The English education system in Ireland has succeeded in making slaves of us. And it has succeeded so well that we no longer realise that we are slaves. Some of us even think our chains ornamental, and are a little doubtful as to whether we shall be quite as comfortable and quite as respectable when they are hacked off ...

A new education system in Ireland has to do more than restore a national culture. It has to restore manhood to a race that has been deprived of it. Along with its inspiration it must, therefore, bring a certain hardening. It must lead Ireland back to her sagas[8] ...

We meet the same ideas, expressed with the same burning conviction though with less violence, in Gandhi:

I am firmly of the view (he said) that the Government schools have unmanned us, rendered us. helpless and Godless[9].

Civilization, in the real sense of the term, consists not in the multi-plication but in the deliberate and voluntary restriction of wants. This alone promotes real happiness and contentment, and increases the capacity for service ...

In my opinion, ... fearlessness is a sine qua non for the growth of other noble qualities. How can one seek Truth or cherish Love, without fearlessness?...

Fear has no place in our hearts when we have shaken off the attachment for wealth, for family and for the body. Enjoy the things of the earth by renouncing them is a noble precept[10].

The Witness of the Ancients

This idea – that pleasure unmans, that manhood is won but by mastery over the appetites, by detachment from those things for which the body craves, that addiction to pleasure is slavery – is no modem brainwave.

It was the central principle in the philosophy of the Stoics who flourished for some centuries before and after Christ and held that virtue is the highest good and that wisdom consists in independence from the passions.

Horace in one of his Epistles tells the story of the horse and the stag that were feeding in a common field. The horse wishing to have the pasture all to himself began a struggle with the stag; but being worsted in the fight he sought the help of man and accepted the bridle and the saddle. Thanks to this ally he worsted his rival. But returning gleefully from his war, he discovered, to his dismay, that he could shake off, alas, neither the bit from his mouth nor the rider from his back!

> Sic qui pauperiem veritus potiore metallis
> Libertate caret, dominum vehit improbus atque
> Serviet aeternum, quia parvo nesciet uti.

> Thus, (warns Horace) he who dreads poverty lacks liberty, (a boon more precious than mines) becomes a covetous wretch and carries a master; and will remain for ever a slave, because he has not learnt to be content with little.

> . . . Fuge magna: licet sub paupere tecto. Reges et regum vita praecurrere amicos.[11]

31

Shun grandeur (he exhorts): beneath a humble roof you may outstrip, in the race of life, kings and friends of kings.

At the start, I brought culture back to its origin and said that as a form of tillage, a higher form at that, the process comprises the action of the tiller, a state induced thereby into the tilled, the growth of the resultant crops and the yield of fruit by these.

There is, however, a difference. In the culture if the vegetable, energy is expended mostly by the tiller; that which is cultivated assumes its state, grows and bears effortlessly. Not so with man as we have seen: the tiller or teacher sweats; the learner as well. There can be no growth in learning or in virtue unless the learner is determined to shun delights and live laborious days. And those who would leave, on departing this life, a name. for science or heroism must give themselves up for years on end to painful and patient drudgery, must die to themselves, as the gospel says.

This proves that the cultural process, by its very nature, calls for sustained effort, calls for manly energy. History shows, again and again, that, when exertion ceases and luxury takes over, decline commences and the knell of a people's greatness begins to toll.

Therefore, nowhere at any time, mould the ideal of manliness be forgotten in the rearing of the young. A people loses sight of this truth to its cost.

If this is so for all nations, how truer still is it for us at this stage of our revolution! To build our country we need armies of citizens equipped to the utmost with knowledge and skill; and the number of such citizens among us is painfully inadequate.

Therefore each Cameroonian we educate today is, ipso facto, destined to be a more efficient tiller of the nation tomorrow, will share in the stupendous task and responsibility of national reconstruction.

If this future participation is to be effective, we must, during the course of his education, give him as motto and din daily into his ears the last admonition which King David, dying, gave to his son Solomon:

> - Esto vir!
> - Be a man[12]

Socrates taught the same doctrine centuries before Christ, namely, that those destined to share public responsibility must be brought up in rigorous discipline:

> Tell me, Aristippus, if it were required of you to take two of your youths and educate them, the one in such a manner that he would be qualified to govern, and the other in such a manner that he would never seek to govern, how would you train them respectively? Will you allow us to consider the matter by commencing with their food, as with the first principles? Food, indeed, replied Aristippus, appears to me one of the first principles,' for a person could not even live if he were not to take food.

> It will be natural for them both, then, said Socrates, to desire to partake of food when a certain hour comes? It will be natural, said Aristippus. And which of the two, then said Socrates, should we accustom to prefer the discharge of any urgent business. to the gratification of his appetite? The one undoubtedly, rejoined Aristippus, who is trained to rule, that the business of the state may not be neglected through his laziness. And on the

same person, continued Socrates, we must, when they desire to drink, impose the duty of being able to endure thirst? Assuredly, replied Aristippus.

And on which of the two should we lay the necessity of being temperate in sleep, so as to be able to go to rest late, to rise early, or 'to remain awake if it should be necessary? Upon the same, doub-tless.

And on which of the two should we impose the obligation to control his sensual appetites, that he may not be hindered by their influence from discharging whatever duty may be required of him? Upon the same.

And on which of the two should we enjoin the duty of not shrinking from labour, but willingly submitting to it? This also is to be enjoined on him who is trained to rule.

And to which of them would it more properly belong to acquire whatever knowledge would assist him to secure the mastery over his rivals? Far more, doubtless, to him who is trained to govern, for without such sort of acquirements there would be no profit in any of his other qualifications.

A man, then, who is thus instructed, would appear to you less liable to be surprised by his enemies than other animals, of which some, we know, are caught by their greediness; and others, though very shy, are yet attracted to the bait by their desire to swallow it, and consequently taken; while others also are entrapped by drink. Indisputably, replied Aristippus.

Are not others, too, caught through their lust, as quails and partridges, which, being attracted to the call of the female by desire and hope of enjoyment, and losing all consideration of danger, fall into traps? To this Aristippus expressed his assent.

Does it not then, proceeded Socrates, appear to you shameful for a man to yield to the same influence as the most senseless of animals,' as adulterers, for instance, knowing that the adulterer is in danger of suffering what the law threatens, and of being watched, and disgraced if caught, yet enter into closets,' and, though there are such dangers and dishonours hanging over the intriguer, and so many occupations that will safely keep him from the desire of sensual gratification, does it not seem to you the part of one tormented with an evil genius, to run, nevertheless, into imminent peril? It does seem so to me, said Aristippus.

And since the greater part of the most necessary employments of life, such as those of war and agriculture, and not a few others, are to be carried on in the open air, does it not appear to you to show great negligence that the majority of mankind should be wholly unexercised to bear cold and heat? Aristippus replied in the affirmative.

Does it not then appear to you that we ought to train him, who is intended to rule, to bear these inconveniences also without difficulty? Doubtless, answered Aristippus.

If therefore, we class those capable of enduring these things among those who are qualified to govern, shall we not class such as are incapable of enduring them among those who will not even aspire to govern? Aristippus expressed his assent[13].

On another occasion, in a discussion with another young man, Socrates dwelt on the same theme:

If there should be occasion to assist our friends or our country, which of the two would have most leisure to attend to such objects, he who lives as I live now, or he who lives, as you think, in happiness?

Which of the two would most readily seek the field of battle, he who cannot exist without expensive dishes, or he who is content with whatever' comes before him?

Which of the two would sooner be reduced by a siege, he who requires what is most difficult to be found, or he who is fully content with what is easiest to be met with?

You, Antipho, resemble one. who thinks that happiness consists in luxury and extravagance; but I think that to want as little as possible is to make the nearest approach to the gods,' that the Divine nature is perfection, and that to be nearest to the Divine nature is to be nearest to perfection.

Back to the Sterner Spirit

The Negro peoples have known the ravages of the Slave Trade and of colonial exploitation; even today, in independent Africa, much of what is rightly ours is still in the hands of the stranger. Indeed the black race is the most despoiled of all mankind. Even among the underdeveloped peoples we can vie with none; our place is right at the bottom. Like the afflicted psalmist, we are struggling to rise **de profundis** – from the depths of the abyss.

Imagine the immensity of the effort that is required of this race to overtake the others, to reach the top!

We rightly assert our equality with other peoples, our equality as human beings, our equality in possibilities of limitless development. But, in so far as real achievement is concerned, all talk of equality is delusive irrelevance, a lullaby for unwary morons.

Indeed when you ponder on how much the Negro must do to catch up with the world, you cannot but be alarmed at the thirst for ease, at the craving for luxury so evident today in independent Africa! This lust for pleasure is rampant precisely where it ought not to venture; it is standing like that **abomination of desolation** which, as the Prophet Daniel lamented, had been **set in the holy places**.

For when you consider the bleak misery in which millions of the African masses pass their lives, you would logically expect that the African elite and leadership, conscious of this state of things, conscious of their responsibilities, and conscious of the need to express genuinely their solidarity with these masses, should be ruled by a stern spirit of self-denial or, at least, of moderate restraint in the acquisition and the use of worldly wealth, especially where they have the sacred duty to develop the common patrimony and use it to alleviate the misery of the people.

Look around you, wherever you may be in Negro Africa, and see for yourself whether this is so.

More often than not what meets your gaze is the same old sight that Tacitus saw among the Romanized Britons – **delenimenta vitiorum: porticus, balinea et conviviorum elegantiam** – the seductions of vice; only among us these assure other shapes: lavish living, luxurious mansions, sumptuous cars, sensual indulgence. The itch to get rich quick is running riot everywhere. No sooner is a bank or exchequer entrusted into African hands than rumours begin to spread of millions spirited away to replenish private coffers.

One can imagine the anguish and bewilderment of many an African head of state caught between this state of things and the relentless clamours for Africanisation. For, Africanise he must, not because Africanisation will usher in efficiency and devoted service, but because we have reached the point where you have no choice but to hand over the African's affairs to the African even when there is every reason to believe that he will make a hash of them.

It is a spectacle disheartening and disturbing. At this stage, when the dawn of African independence is just breaking, evils which would normally come with decline and exhaustion have already overtaken us and are eating their way deep into the vitals of the body politic-corruption, embezzlement, nepotism, grasping individualism, cynical indifference to the general welfare.

A halt must be called to this down-hill trend. There must be a radical reversal. Nothing short of a complete mental and moral revolution will do.

Behind the giant effort to establish colleges and universities throughout the continent there pulses the driving conviction that, to pull Africa out of the bottomless pit, we need men of high learning and specialised skill. This is obviously so.

But it would be an omission fraught with disaster if we failed to make sure that these saviours of Africa are drilled in self-discipline, are forged like steel into men of stoic mind and will. For indeed, seeing the extreme misery of the African masses, how can those dedicated to the cause of redeeming these masses fulfil this mission duly, if they recoil from Calvary, if they shrink back from descending into hell? The situation calls for the spirit of self-sacrifice, indeed it calls for austere asceticism, in the lives of the African elite and leadership.

If they are not fortified ill this manner with a will of iron, they will stand in constant danger of being caught in the toils of the wily imperialist who is ever scheming to use his lavish means to enkindle the greed and the lusts of the elite in order to make them traitors to the trust of their people.

Without a leadership drilled in self-denial and trained to be generous, political systems, however perfect on paper, will do us no good. For, where the elite is heartless, grasping and given to self-indulgence, whether the regime in power is frankly reactionary or whether it wears a socialist cloak, the result will be the same – misery for the many, luxury for the few; the creation and the entrenchment on this continent of two embittered, mutually-hating Africas, with all the explosive forces that this state of things is sure to set smouldering.

We are striving and straining, as is our duty, to put all the new learn-ing that the white man has brought at the disposal of our children. We rightly regard it as absolutely indispensable for our welfare and progress today.

But that is not enough!

An education system in which intensive intellectual training is counterbalanced by a moral training equally intensive is the most effective means of producing the type of man needed today in Africa.

We know the ceaseless drudgery involved in the very nature of the work of tilling the faculties of man; we know the staggering efforts demanded particularly from the Negro peoples and we know the harm that has been wrought in them by colonial emasculation.

Therefore, if these enormous difficulties shall be overcome; if we shall accomplish effectively that phase of the cultural process which consists in action, in the tilling of man; if we shall charge our youth with really genuine manliness; if we shall forge more efficient tillers for the Cameroon of tomorrow; if we shall foster genius among us and help it to enrich our cultural heritage with achievements that will last; – then our new education system must do more than steep our children in the modem arts and in the modem sciences: it must restore manhood to a race unmanned; it must entail, therefore, a good deal of hardening; it must lead us back to the spirit of the initiation days; back to the fundamental principle that one of the principal ends of education is to teach man to fight – to fight against external foes; to fight for the right against the wrong; and, above all else, to fight against himself, against his restive passions, to drill himself in disci-pline.

Recently, the renowned Negro poet, Aime Cesaire, came out with a very meaningful play: **La tragedie du Roi Christophe.** As its title indicates, it deals with the reign of the Emperor Henry Christopher of Haiti who ruled that first of independent Negro states from 1811 to 1820. Toussaint Louverture, the legendary revolutionary hero, had led the slaves against the French from 1796 till he was captured, taken to France and cast into the dungeon at Joux where he died in 1802. Jean Jacques Dessalines took over and won independence for Haiti in 1804, the second independence to be gained in the Western Hemisphere, next only to that of the United States. Henry Christopher ruled during a period similar to that through which most of Africa is going today-the period immediately following independence; the period when so many believe that they should eat, drink and make merry when, indeed, what the situation calls for, precisely, is redoubled effort. In fact, behind Haiti and the Emperor Christopher, Cesaire is really dealing with the problems that beset the African people and their leadership, today, just after independence.

One of he characters accuses Christopher of being too hard on the people. And he makes indignant answer:

> That I ask too much of men! No, not enough, when you consider that it is of blackmen.
> If there is anything which gets as much on my nerves as the language of slave masters, it is to hear our philanthropists proclaim loudly, and of course with the best of intentions, that all men are men, that there is neither white nor black. This is arm-chair theorising, out of touch with reality.
>
> All men have the same rights. I agree. But of the common lot some have more duties than others. There you have inequality. The inequality of imperatives.
>
> Whom would you convince that all men, I say all, without privilege, without any exception whatsoever, have known deportation, have been bought and sold, have been collectively lowered to the level of the beast, have known

outrage without limit, insult without measure,
have been spat upon right into their faces with
that all-denying contempt! We alone... yes... we
alone, blackmen.

Indeed, it is at the bottom of the pit, at the very lowest
part of it, that we are yearning for air and light and sun.

And if we would rise, ours must be the foot set with the
firmness of a buttress; ours must be the muscle exerted
taut, the teeth clenched tight, ours must be a head large,
yes, large and cold.

There you see why more must be demanded from
Negroes than from others: more work, more faith, more zest;
one step and then another; each step a victory won! I speak
of an upward strain-ing such as the world has never seen.
And woe to him who winces[14]!

Part Two
Culture as Fruit and Harvest

In the first part of this article, I considered culture as tillage and I said that it comprises, firstly, the action of the tiller, secondly, the state of refinement induced by that action into that which is tilled, thirdly, the growth that diligent tending and the state of cultivation promote in the plant, and fourthly, the fruit that is borne by this plant thanks to action, state and growth. Culture considered as action, is suffered by the subject, considered as state, is inherent in that subject, but culture considered as the fruit yielded by cultivated humanity, the enduring content of human civilization, is a tertium quid distinct from man, it survives him and is handed down from generation to generation.

It is this last aspect of culture that we will proceed to consider. As I said before, every cultural element takes its birth from 8 specific human need. And, as man is a compound of flesh, sense, mind and will, there are definite elements of culture that have been created as a result of the needs of each of these components of he human being.

The Physical Strata

At the level of the flesh, the most basic needs of man are for food, clothing and shelter. To obtain these, man needs to know, to dominate and alter the materiel universe. To overmaster and transform the universe, to bring about motion and change, man has been engaged, from the beginning of his existence, in the quest for energy. It is this quest for energy excited in man by the need to allay his physical hunger, to slake his physical thirst, to shield himself against the inclement elements that has given rise to all the inventions of the physical sciences, from the discovery of fire to the fission of the atom, from the invention of the wheel to that of the space-crafts thanks to which the conquest of space and of the planets will become a reality.

It is the material need of man that has given rise to that section of culture that is composed by the impressive galaxy of the natural and the physical sciences.

The Strata of the Arts

Furthermore, man is able to establish contact with the world by means of his senses, and, in turn, the impact of the world on these senses stirs up in him feelings of pleasure or pain, love or hate, desire or aversion, joy or sorrow, hope or despair, daring or fear, revolt or submission.

Thus, for instance, the cravings of touch and taste and smell impel man to look for ways and means of improving his food he wants it tasty and fragrant; of improving his clothing and shelter-he wants them cosy, cool or warm. And thus, gradually, men have arrived at the exquisite refinements of the culinary, the textile and the architectural arts.

Similarly, the need to charm the ear with sound and rhythm, melody and harmony, the need to delight the eye with colour and shape, to enchant the imagination with imagery and association, and the need to rouse and soothe the emotions have enriched the world with music and sculpture and painting and literature.

The Strata of Abstract Thought

But man, as we have seen, is not merely flesh to be fed and feeling to be thrilled. He is tormented by thirsts and voids, not only at the level of flesh and sense, but also at the level of his mind. He is tormented by a hundred whys and wherefores about himself and about the world: what is the nature of the universe? What is the ultimate composition of being? What is the final classification of things? What are the ultimate principles of becoming, of motion and change? What is quantity? What is space? What is time? What is mind? What is the nature of knowledge? What is the final end of life? What is the ultimate norm of morality? These are the questions that have led to the elaboration of the various systems of philosophy, from the time of Thales to the present day.

The Primacy of Morality

Yet, even when a man feeds on the daintiest dishes and is clothed in silk and purple and is satiated with the delights of sound and song, of colour and shape; even if he has dug to the bottom of the mysteries of the universe, he still finds, after all these achievements, that his mind is not yet satisfied.

For his reason sheds a light on things, shows some up as good and right, and shows some up as evil and wrong. Within him he feels that he is master of himself and can do as he pleases. But up against these two alternatives, good and evil, right and wrong, he hears a soft but inflexible voice within him commanding that what is good must be chosen, and what is evil avoided; that what is right must be done, what is wrong must be shunned.

Two *things fill* my soul *with* awe, declared *the* celebrated German *Philosopher, Immanuel* Kant, two *things fill my* soul *with* awe and *with* a veneration *that* renews *itself* and *increases* as *mind* returns to *them* and ponders *them* over more and more: *the starry skies* above *us, the moral law within us, do not* need to *make them the object* of *search* or *surmise* as *if they* were *shrouded in mist and held beyond my horizon, in* a *region inaccessible. I* see *them before* me *and I link them immediately with the consciousness* of *my existence.*

Choose the good and reject the evil, love the right and hate the *wrong,* this is the first principle of morality, the **Categorical Imperative,** as Kant was wont to call it, that each man sees as self-evident as soon as reason dawns.

Difficulties and differences arise only when it comes to specify in the concrete and in detail what is evil, what is good; what is wrong, what is right.

It is from this simple origin that have evolved the multitudinous morals and manners of the human race.

From it as starting point, the more daring among men are led by their reason up the rugged heights of more heroic morality:

> To every man there openeth
> A way and ways and a way.
>
> And the High Soul climbs the High Way
> And the Low Soul gropes the Low,
> And, in between, on the misty flats,
> The rest drift to and fro.
>
> And to every man there openeth
> A high Way and a Low
> And every man decideth
> The Way his Soul shall go.

It is the ability not only to reason but to distinguish right from wrong, to freely do the one and shun the other that makes man, as Lord Tennyson:

> "The roof and crown of things"[15]

Furthermore, among men, it is heroic conduct that raises a given individual head and shoulders above the common run.

Of all the things that humans crave for, as the highest good – abundant wealth, physical prowess, fineness of feeling, pleasure mental and material, profound learning, political power – therefore, the highest place, in the natural order of things, must be given to those values which, because they are abstract, spiritual, have been termed by some as the **imponderables,** those values, which, when embodied in a human life, make an upright virtuous man.

Let men say what they please, the fact will remain, for ever, that things like truthfulness, justice, purity of life, conquest of self, heroism, fidelity to duty at all costs, count before everything, are the foundation, the safeguards, without which no society can escape disaster. In other words, morality holds the primacy in all the affairs of men. Witness the high esteem with which men of outstanding virtue have been held all through the ages. Great inventors to whom the modern world owes almost everything, great scholars, great law-makers, great heroes in war, are rightly venerated in all places and all times.

But men of exceptional moral doctrine and virtue have always been treated, by mankind, with especial awe.

Witness the tremendous influence that the world's great teachers of sublime moral principles have wielded and will continue to wield, as long as men exist and history is unbroken: Christ, Gautama the Buddha, Socrates, Mohammed.

In our own day, the veneration with which Mahatma Gandhi was held by millions the world over is still a living memory. And among the statesmen of the world of our times there was hardly one treated with greater worship, by so many millions, as the Pandit, Jawaharlal Nehru. For the Indians knew his record; they knew that Nehru would never let them down, would never deceive them; that Nehru lived only for them; they knew that, if it came to dying, Nehru would die for them.

If you admit this point of view, you will go on to admit as well that the essential greatness of a nation does not consist in the extent of its territory, in the abundance of its wealth, or in the vastness of its population. There is no contesting the importance of these, as far as they go. But they are external, material. The intrinsic greatness of a country, the genuine greatness of a nation, lies in the character of its people.

If this is true, then we must go on to conclude that a nation's highest cultural achievement can be no other thing but the degree of the excellence of the system of morals and manners that it has evolved to enable its children to acquire such a character, to enable them to live lives worthy of that which is highest and best in man.

We rightly admire and should duly salute the unspeakable achievements of the whiteman's culture in the field of science and technological know-how. And whatever be our zeal, whatever be our will, to vindicate and restore the culture of our ancestors, our determination and our effort to learn these skills and make them our own should not relent for once. We have before us only two choices: to master these skills and master them fast and master them thoroughly, and build upon them – or to remain for ever slaves.

And yet however over-awing the appearances, we must never forget that there is a hierarchy in human values which hierarchy is not determined by appearances. Technical skill and science, for all their overwhelming importance are but means to an end, servant to master, and therefore cannot be given the primacy. They are meant to help man to become more and more a man, that is, to acquire increasing moral excellence.

In fact, when we look back at some of the things that the whiteman has done with his superior knowledge, there is every reason to fear lest these skills may end by making man return into the beast-and a wilder and more vicious one at that. For Science and Technical skill in the hands of a thief and liar can only make him a finer and more efficient thief and liar.

The discovery or the possession of these tremendous powers, therefore, does not confer, ipso facto, genuine human greatness. They can make it, they can merit. And whether they make or mar, depends upon their use or abuse – on the presence and the observance, or the absence, of sound moral principles.

In fact, to-day, it is a very naive whiteman who still expects the under-privileged world to look at his race with wide-eyed admiration. For when these under-privileged, long the victims of exploitation, think of such things as the African Slave Trade, imperialist colonialism, the anti-Semitic atrocities of the Third Reich and twentieth century warfare, they cannot help but see that in the hands of the whiteman superior knowledge and skill, alas, have been put, quite often in history, at the service of monstrous lying, phenomenal injustice and unspeakable wickedness. It is a record for which every thinking whiteman should hang his head in shame.

The Unerring Test of Civilisation

Furthermore there is in man, as we know only too well, the irrepressible impulse to perpetuate his kind; and this has given rise to marriage and to the diverse systems designed to give stability to this all-important instruction.

In like manner, the need for mutual help and protection has led to the rise of human communities – the family, the state, the nation. And once a community comes into being, be it ever so small, there is felt the need for authority – order must be maintained, respect of rights and fulfilment of obligations enforced, recalcitrant members disciplined, for the good of all. Thus arises, government with its threefold power – the power to make laws, the power to put them into effect, and the power to judge and punish. It is this threefold authority that finds embodiment in legislative, executive and judiciary institutions, things of primordial worth in any cultural set-up.

Indeed, in determining a nation's rank in cultural evolution no test is more decisive than the degree to which justice is actually realised in its judicial administration both as between one private citizen and another and as between private citizens and members of the government.

The Role of Religion

Having the wherewithal to supply his body's needs, having tasted to his soul's desire of the pleasures of sense and mind, having unearthed the mysteries of the nature of the universe and of the nature of man, having laid down laws and manners to guide his individual and corporate conduct, man remains, notwithstanding, still unsatisfied.

He looks at this marvellous world, at his own unfathomable self and asks in bewilderment: Whence? Whither? Why? For these must have an origin, a destiny and a purpose.

And thus begins the genesis and the growth of the numerous religious systems with their creeds, rules and rituals; thus arises the idea of a God, the origin and the end of the universe, maker of the moral law, rewarder of the good, punisher of the wicked, father of all men to whom they return after their sojourn through the world.

It is this universal belief that Schiller celebrated in his famous hymn, **An die Freude**, a poem which Beethoven rendered immortal by his Choral Symphony:

> Seid umschlungen, Millionen!
> Diesen Kuss der ganzen Welt!
> Briider-ûberm Sternenzelt
> Muss ein lieber Vater wohnen.
> "Embrace yourselves, ye Millions! This kiss of
> the entire world!

Brothers, above the starry canopy, there must
dwell a loved Father."

Duldet mutig, Millionen!
Duldet fûr die bessre Welt!
Droben ûberm Sternenzeft
Wird ein grosser Gott belohnen.
"Suffer with courage, ye Millions! Suffer for a
better world.
There above the starry skies shall a greater God
reward you."

Religion reinforces morality by instilling into men the
love of a universal father and the fear of supernatural
sanctions. Thus the importance of religion as a cultural
element needs no belabouring. The number of men and
women that have laid down their lives in its defence, right
through the ages, is legion; for, often, in history, men have
been ready to die not only *pro focis* –for their hearths and
homes, but oftener still *pro aris* – for their altars and shrines.

I have said above that, in the natural order of things,
morality, as a constituent part of culture, takes the primacy.
But when we cease to think of man alone and consider the
universe in its totality, when we consider together both the
natural and the supernatural order, the material and the
spiritual, we are bound to yield supremacy to religion. For
if God is the creator, the beginning and the end of the
universe, then that which concerns knowledge and worship
of him must be supreme. If it is true that man has a
supernatural final destiny, which is union with God, and
that he can attain unalloyed and endless happiness only in
this union, then the means to attain this end must constitute
the highest duty of man. As a matter of historical fact, the
greatest civilizations that the world has seen – Bhuddhism,
Christianity, Islam – have religion as their essence.

Furthermore, not even the staunchest, the most obdurate atheist can contest the primordial role that religion has played not only as a cultural element in itself but also as a force for cultural advancement at all levels: architecture, sculpture, painting, music, literature, philosophy, the spread of learning – each of these fields can show realisations of the highest merit to attest the truth of this assertion.

African folk are deeply religious folk and much of African culture takes its birth from religious inspiration.

Summing Up

To sum up therefore: wherever there is a human need to satisfy, a human craving to allay, wherever a skill or system has been evolved for that purpose, there you have a cultural element.

The natural and the physical sciences elaborated for the knowledge and the conquest of the concrete universe to supply the bodily needs of man constitute the material strata of culture.

Scaling higher rungs we come to the aesthetic realm of culture – architecture, sculpture, painting, music, literature – where feelings are roused and soothed through the perception and the contemplation, by sense and mind, of the harmony of shape, colour, sound and thought, and of heroic and sublime conduct and cha-racter. Higher still we attain the elevated strata of philosophy.

And finally we reach the realm where morals and law and virtue and religion strive to tame the refractory will in man, to make him live as he should, that is, a being governed by reason and faith. For man is a union of the sublime and the earthy, beast and angel both in one, or, as a writer put it (speaking of the poet Burns): half dust, half deity[16].

And what higher duty can he have than to curb the beast and give the angel victory, to raise the low, and make the dust divine?

These cultural divisions, which I have based on the faculties of man, are only meant to shed light on this question; for there are no water-tight compartments in human life; and although there is a hierarchy in human values, these values are all inter-dependent, are meant to serve one final end, namely, the up-lift and the cultivation of man and the attainment of happiness. Moreover, behind all cultural activity there is but one supreme, master architect – the human mind.

As I observed earlier, the fundamental needs of man are the same for all men; and, if men were all supremely perfect in mind and will there would be but only one culture the world over. But the intellect, man's instrument for the fashioning of culture, is imperfect, human inclinations are corrupt, there are differences of place and time, differences of means, inequalities in development; these are the factors responsible for the diversity and the imperfections of the cultures of the world.

There are, therefore, from various points of view, advanced cultures and backward cultures. Thus, to-day, while the African peasant has nothing to carry him around but his two weary limbs, the whiteman is soaring into the heavens and heading for the moon.

I say "from various points of view" because it does not follow that a culture which excels in one thing has a monopoly of excellence in everything, nor that, because a culture is backward, it is destitute of excellence in all respects.

The Principles of Cultural Growth

With regard to cultural growth and development, I have already said that, where nature is generous, where the tooth of want is not so keen, where only the minimum of effort is required for needs to be supplied, where men are untroubled by doubt and deaf to the urgings of the spirit of inquiry, minds remain compla-cent and beclouded and cultural achievement cannot be impressive.

On the contrary, where nature subjects man to extremes of climate, where men have to think hard and exert their minds to the utmost to fend for themselves, cultural achievement has been great. Furthermore, in the fields of scientific invention, artistic creativeness, the advancement of social institutions, moral perfection, where individuals or communities are not satisfied with present achievements but are animated by ideals which they ceaselessly strive to attain, cultural progress has been continuous and rapid. In the scientific and philosophical fields, where men's minds are in doubt with regard to the certainty of their tenets, where the urge to inquire is for ever gnawing, there too cultural achievement and progress have been fast and impressive. In like manner, when a people is neighbour to another whose cultural achievement they can imitate or emulate, there too cultural progress has been great. Where there is a government tolerant of new or critical ideas, and eager to advance creative effort, science and social institutions, there culture is sure to make steady, impressive progress. Furthermore, where there is peace, where resources are abundant and where men are not completely absorbed in the struggle for the merest subsistence, there culture can advance with rapid strides. In brief, the sting of want, the changing inclemency of nature, the inspiration of lofty ideals, philosophical doubt, the spirit of inquiry, contact with more advanced cultures, freedom and peace, abundant wealth and leisure – these are the factors conducive to cultural growth.

Culture and Africa

For a long time there was doubt and debate as to whether there existed such a thing as African Culture, African History? Whether the Negro people, like the white or the yellow, had a past worthy of pride?

To-day, no such debate can be entertained by serious scholarship; for, to-day, archaeology is revealing, to all who care to look, the stupendous glories of the Negro's past.

Let us forget about Egypt, although the black man can claim, and with rich justification, to have shared, in no small measure, in the creation of the civilization that has made the banks of the Nile unique in the history of the world. Let us concentrate our attention on authentic, undisputed Negro Africa. Taking a few random samples, as we move from west to east, we meet Ghana, Mali and Songhay in the Western Sudan, Nok in the Central, Meroe in the Eastern Sudan, and Zimbabwe, further to the south-east, in what they call Rhodesia.

About Ghana, Mali and Song hay, the fabulous Negro Empires that flourished in the Middle Ages, so much has been said and so much is known that there is no need to dwell on them unduly.

Ancient Ghana's wealth was so abundant that this country won for itself the title of the Land of Gold. In the middle of the eleventh century, its history was well documented by the North African writer Abdalla Ibn Abdel Aziz more familiarly known as EI Bekri. Writing in 1067, EI Bekri asserted that the king of Ghana could put 200,000 warriors on the field, more than 40,000 of whom were archers. The rest were most probably spearmen. Obviously, the cavalry formed a substantial portion of this army. 1067 – that was just one year after William the Conqueror crossed the Channel with some 10,000 troops, knights and the footmen, and took Anglo-Saxon England. One is led to speculate what would have been the issue if William of Normandy had pitted his forces against the Ghana Emperor instead of against King Harold England. But there can be no debate on this that, for wealth and might and splendour, the two European antagonists were no match for the Negro Empire.

Mali which followed Ghana was certainly the richest realm in' Africa, and perhaps in the world, in its time. A sign of this wealth was the dazzling Ha]] that the Mansa or Emperor, Kongo Musa, made to Mecca in 1324. He took with him a caravan of 60,000 people and about 100 camel loads of gold each weighing about 300 pounds. It was the biggest moving crowd that Africa had ever seen. And the spectacular wealth that this has displayed so dazzled the people in his line of march that their descendant still talked about it a hundred years after.

During the Mali and the Songhay Empires, learning flourished in the Western Sudan. Timbuktu, for instance, was famous for its **Sankore** or university which attracted students from far and wide in Africa. Jenne was another centre of learning which boasted of a university where not only lectures were given but research was carried on.

A revolutionary and far reaching influence in the rise and the spread of these civilizations was the use of iron. Iron ore was plentiful, and tools and weapons made from it were far more effective, in work and war, than those made from copper, 'bronze, stone or wood. Iron gave mastery over soil and forest, over stone and bone and wood-using neighbours; it gave ease to conquest, and, thus, to the establishment of centralised government, and, thereby, to the promotion of new forms of social organization.

To the eastward, archaeologists have unearthed a culture that is estimated to date from 3,000 years before Christ. The world got the first hint of the existence of this culture from the discovery, in 1931, of a few human heads in pottery in the village of Nok[17] in Zaria Province in Northern Nigeria. Since then, many more specimens of this art have been found in the wide area extending for some 300 miles across the broad valley that runs from east to west above the confluence of the Niger and the Benue. Among these specimens there are many portrait heads, stylistically modelled. Furthermore, it is asserted that Nok culture was of revo-lutionary significance, because it was the earliest iron-using culture in these parts of Africa. It is also thought to have given rise to further developments in art, social organization and religion. The discovery of the Nok portrait heads proved that, contrary to what deep-seated European prejudice was wont to believe, Negro peo-ples possessed an ancient and authentic native tradition in anthropomorphic art, that is, the more or less naturalistic portrayal of humanity. For, indeed, when the first astonishing heads and busts were brought to Europe, at the dawn of this century, from Ife and Benin they were greeted by a chorus of disbelief: surely they were Portuguese, Egyptian or Greek but certainly not Negro. Utterly impossible! How could niggers be capable of such things!

To-day, however, further discoveries in the Sahara have revealed that Negro peoples were painting men and! women with sensitive realism 3,000 years before Christ, and, that they were, perhaps, among the originators of naturalistic portraiture.

Further to the eastward, in what is now the Republic of Sudan, and north of present-day Khartoum, lies the area where, some 2,000 years or so ago, lay the Empire of Kush[18]. Near the sixth cataract of the Nile, a hundred miles from what is now Khartoum, was situated, in those days, the

Kushite capital of Meroe. As archaeological investigation progresses, it is being established that its ruins are among the great monuments of the ancient world; indeed these Kushite ruins, of which only a tiny portion has been explored, are declared to constitute the richest archaeological sight that still remains in Africa, and, perhaps, the richest that still remains in any part of the world. At Meroe, and at other parts of what was ancient Kush, stand solitary ruins of palaces and temples that must have been built for a civilization that flowered, as I have said above, more than 2,000 years ago.

Southward from the Sudan, we move down to Rhodesia, and, in the area below the town of Fort Victoria, are scattered the stone ruins known as the Great Zlmbebwe[19]. They have their fame and reputation among many -ruins in Rhodesia for their skilful putting together, their large conception, their tall girdling walls and towers, their rounded gateways, their evidence of power and unity and ordered settlement. The European explorers who first saw Zimbabwe could not believe that the forebears of the uncouth, hut-dwelling Africans whom they met had built these stone walls and massive palaces. But the more these ruins are investigated, the more evident it becomes that they must have sprung from the native craftsmanship and ingenuity of peoples who worked without any outside architectural influence to guide or help them. Everywhere these structures are marked by an originality which seems to owe nothing to the rest of the world.

Such was the grandeur of ancient Africa.

And lest you accuse me of partiality or exaggeration, let me say that it is not I that am singing the praises of old Africa; it is the Egyptologist, Dr. Jean Vercoutter, it is William Fagg and Griffith; it is Basil Davidson from whom I have drawn a deal, it is Reisner and Garstang, it is the French, English, German archaeologists and scholars who are bearing witness. For, for the most part, at least for the present, the Africans have neither the resources, nor the know-how, nor the leisure for vast and prolonged archaeological investigations. It is the whiteman's mouth, lately foul and strident with insult, abuse and contempt against the black, that is to-day sweet and loud in the proclamation of the glory of our dusky forefathers.

I have said and stressed elsewhere that culture, essentially and before all else, is thought, scientific and philosophic thought, thought that grows from cause to effect. Consequently, where there are great or revolutionary realisations in science, in the arts, in advanced social institutions, there must be a great culture; for such realisations, as a matter of metaphysical necessity, must arise from great and organised ideas and principles, from systems of thought. That ancient Africa, therefore, possessed great cultures, at all levels, is a fact firmly established to-day and put, completely forever, outside the arena of scientific controversy.

The Decline and the Cause

Yet not even the most rabid of African nationalists will dispute the fact that present-day Negro culture, in comparison with the pristine glories of Africa, is obviously poor.

What was it then that brought a blight on this splendour? The answer is not far to seek.

I said before that among the factors conductive towards cultural growth, either through internal evolution, independent invention and creation or through contact with external cultures richer by reason of greater achievement, are freedom, peace and leisure.

But from the beginning of the sixteenth century to our own day, without respite, there was to be no freedom, no peace and no leisure for Negro Africa. It was an unbroken period of unrelenting warfare, deluvial destruction and down-grinding slavery.

For the conquest of the New World, as everybody knows, took place before the scientific and industrial revolution. Then only brawn could exploit the new and limitless wealth; and the only brawn that was found abundant and suitable was Negro brawn. And so began the devastation, the unprecedented spoliation and the diaspora of the Negro race.

For four hundred years the blackman was hunted down like' a beast throughout Africa; and the flower of Negro manhood was carried off to America; and everywhere the blackman went, he met with nothing but unrelieved tribulation. Four hundred years – just imagine that! Four hundred years of relentless butchery, rapine, wholesale destruction, terror, untold cruelty, commotion, chaos, disaster! Can you find anything to parallel this, for vastness and intensity, anywhere in the History of mankind?

How could culture survive and grow in such an atmosphere of protracted turbulence? How can society flourish where hell is let loose? Do you still wonder then at the blighted state of present-clay African culture? Rather you should wonder that anything remained at all! Indeed there are serious writers, not Africans, who have argued to the Negro's superiority from the fact that he was able to survive such unspeakable catastrophes. For where is the Caribbean to-clay? Where the American Indian?

The end of slavery, however, did not mean the end of the Negro's woes; for it yielded place almost immediately to imperialist colonialism and to racial discrimination. The whiteman strove, might and main, to despoil the black on his own continent, of his own continent, strove to keep him down lest he should rise and become a rival. And to make this new implacable thraldom more complete, they decided to enslave his soul, to inculcate into his mind, through raillery and contempt the idea that he was inherently despicable and inferior and that all excellence, all nobility, all that is beautiful and sublime was white. And thus they were able to make him detest himself and the works of his hands.

Restoring the Remnants

B ut, fortunately, not everything was destroyed. In the arts, in the field of moral and social values, much remains that merits l to be admired and preserved. African sculpture, as everybody knows, has been an inspiration to modern European art. There exists in Africa a wealth of unrecorded traditional literature. The African tendency to give primacy to human, social, moral and spiritual considerations, as opposed to calculations of materiel gain or advantage, should be encouraged and reinforced. The straightforward candour, the simplicity and the naturalness of the African's attitude towards his fellow men is to be preferred to the artificiality, the excessive cultivation, the sophistication and the over-fineness of European manners. The African conviction that the inculcation of manliness is a first principle of education should be restored and stressed in the face of the emasculating effects of pleasure loving western materialism. The spirit of African solidarity as the foundation and the bond of society must be protected, preserved and consolidated against the blight and the disintegrating effects of European individualism.

There does exist, therefore, an African culture worthy of preservation. Furthermore, it is to be stressed that, in despite of intensive efforts at westernisation, this traditional culture remains the way of life of the vast majority of the African peoples, and that it constitutes the warp and woof of the thought of the said peoples.

It is not therefore possible, were it even desirable, to raze this culture to the ground and to begin afresh to build on a new and foreign basis. From the very nature of things, therefore, account must be taken of African culture in the erection of the new African cultural edifice.

In support of this thesis, Aime Cesaire, the renowned West Indian Negro poet, once said that the shortest and safest road to the future lies through the past. In other words, we would know cock-surely whither we should tend, if we knew as surely whence we have come. Furthermore, in teaching, it is laid down, as a first principle, that surest instruction goes from known to unknown, from within without, from home abroad.

The culture that we have inherited from the past, therefore, must be the foundation on which the modern African cultural structure should be raised; the soil into which the new seed should be sown; the stem into which the new scion should be grafted; the sap that should enliven the entire organism.

As I have said before, this culture was the object of imperialist mockery, it was despised and rejected; our first and primordial duty to-clay, therefore, in its regard, is to rehabilitate it. This advocation of the restauration of African culture must be accompanied, however, by a word of warning.

The rehabilitation of African culture cannot be a mere archaeological enterprise; it will not answer to dig up the past and live it as it was. For, for one thing, like any other work of the hands of man, African culture is not without its imperfections; for another, times change and African culture must adapt itself, at every turn, to the changing times.

In restoring African culture, therefore, we must steer clear of two extremes: on the one hand, the imperialist arrogance which declared everything African as only fit for the scrap-heap and the dust-bin, and, on the other hand, the overly enthusiastic and rather naive tendency to laud every aspect of African culture as if it were the quintessence of human achievement.

There is, in the hymn to the Holy Spirit, in the Catholic Service for Pentecost Sunday, a passage which, to my mind, expresses very aptly what should be our policy on this important point of cultural rehabilitation:

> Lava quod est sordidum,
> riga quod est aridum,
> sana quod est sancium;
> fJecte quod est frigidum,
> fove quod est frigidum,
> rege quod es devium.

> Cleanse the sordid,
> water the arid,

> heal the wounded;
> render the rigid pliant,
> make the frigid warm,
> and the crooked straight.

For, if this rehabilitation is to be worth the while, it must result in a culture shorn and purged of all that is filthy; it must be rendered fertile in order to foster growth, invention, and creative activity; it must pulse with health and vigour in all its members. Furthermore, while remaining true and faithful to itself, it must be flexible, easily readjustable to the reasonable exigencies of time and place; it must be rich with the genuine warmth of generous humanity and must walk the straight and narrow road of truth and justice.

The work of cultural rehabilitation in Africa, therefore, must be, not a work of indiscriminate restoration, but one of critical and judicious selection.

Furthermore, rehabilitating African culture is not the same thing as building a museum where the best realisations of the past are preserved and exposed for admiration. Culture, as I have said before, is something organic, something living, something which grows and which sometimes undergoes changes that are tantamount to a very metamorphosis. What a world separates the ancient Roman cart from the supersonic airliner, the mediaeval knight's armour from the modern jet-fighter armed with nuclear warheads! But European civilization claims them both.

It would be misleading therefore to maintain that the only authentic elements of African culture are those inherited from the past. On the contrary, any Invention, any creation that is the genuine outcome of African genius, effort and initiative, however new-fangled it may look, is really and truly African.

Indeed, any African who saw the dawn of this century and whom age preserves to see its close, will have witnessed, in his time, a very metamorphosis in African culture; and, in the twilight of his days, even among his own people, he may feel himself:

> "... *companionless, Among* new men, strange faces, *other minds.*"[20]

Yet, both he the wizened relic of the century's dawn about whom the days and years darken and the strange young men of the rising age with the new manners, other minds, will be both authentic, genuine Africans.

Therefore, to the imperious duty of promoting judicious cultural restoration and rehabilitation must be added the equally imperious one of fostering cultural growth. This growth, this development, can be achieved and kept up, as we have seen before, through internal and independent cultural evolution, invention, creation, according as circumstances change and new needs and challenges arise.

On the other hand, it can also be realised, as I have said already, through fruitful contact with more advanced cultures. For just as a living organism can take in dead external matter-animal vegetable, mineral, gaseous-and digest it, and transform it, and absorb it into its own flesh and blood in such wise that both become one and indistinguishable, in the same manner, whenever a genuine need exists, the culture that feels this need can supply it by borrowing from wealthier neighbours and by so thoroughly digesting and absorbing the new cultural acquisitions that they become part and parcel of the substance of its being.

And here it is that an important question comes in, namely, that of Cultural Integration. To-day, this question, as I said at the start, has become the urgent problem, the rousing challenge, a burning need in Africa.

Notes

1. Alfred Lord Tennyson: The Idylls of the Kind: The coming of King Arthur.

2. TuscuI, V. 10

3. De Consolatione, III, 2

4. la, Q. 26, al

5. Satura, X; I, 356

6. Tacitus-Agricola xxx.

7. Tacitus-Agricola XXI.

8. Padraic Pearse-Political Writings and Speeches, pp 6... 41.

9. Mahatma Gandhi's Ideas by C. F. Andrews, p. 266.

10. Mahatma Gandhi: Selected Writings: Ronald Dancan-p. 47, 49, 50.

11. Epistles 1,10

12. (Vulgate) III Kings 2,2.

13. Socratic Discourses: Plato and Xenophon pp. 32. 35-37.

14. Aime Cesaire La Tragedie du Roi Christophe, pages 61-62.

15. Alfred Lord Tennyson: The *Lotus Eaters*.

16. *Pictures from English Literature*, p.86.

17. Basil Davidson-Old *Africa Rediscovered*, pages 65-66.

18. Basil Davidson: *Old Africa Rediscovered*, pages 50-57.

19. Basil Davidson: *Old Africa Rediscovered*, pages 203-205.

20. Lord Tennyson: Morte d'Arthur.

Titles by *Langaa* RPCIG

Jude Fokwang
Mediating Legitimacy: Chieftaincy and Democratisation in Two African Chiefdoms

Michael A. Yanou
Dispossession and Access to Land in South Africa: an African Perspevctive

Tikum Mbah Azonga
Cup Man and Other Stories
The Wooden Bicycle and Other Stories

John Nkemngong Nkengasong
Letters to Marions (And the Coming Generations)
The Call of Blood

Amady Aly Dieng
Les étudiants africains et la littérature négro-africaine d'expression française

Tah Asongwed
Born to Rule: Autobiography of a life President
Child of Earth

Frida Menkan Mbunda
Shadows From The Abyss

Bongasu Tanla Kishani
A Basket of Kola Nuts
Konglanjo (Spears of Love without Ill-fortune) and Letters to Ethiopia with some Random Poems

Fo Angwafo III S.A.N of Mankon
Royalty and Politics: The Story of My Life

Basil Diki
The Lord of Anomy
Shrouded Blessings

Churchill Ewumbue-Monono
Youth and Nation-Building in Cameroon: A Study of National Youth Day Messages and Leadership Discourse (1949-2009)

Emmanuel N. Chia, Joseph C. Suh & Alexandre Ndeffo Tene
Perspectives on Translation and Interpretation in Cameroon

Linus T. Asong
The Crown of Thorns
No Way to Die
A Legend of the Dead: Sequel of *The Crown of Thorns*
The Akroma File
Salvation Colony: Sequel to *No Way to Die*
Chopchair
Doctor Frederick Ngenito
The Crabs of Bangui

Vivian Sihshu Yenika
Imitation Whiteman
Press Lake Varsity Girls: The Freshman Year

Beatrice Fri Bime
Someplace, Somewhere
Mystique: A Collection of Lake Myths

Shadrach A. Ambanasom
Son of the Native Soil
The Cameroonian Novel of English Expression: An Introduction
Education of the Deprived: Anglophone Cameroon Literary Drama
Homage and Courtship *(Romantic Stirrings of a Yourng Man)*

Tangie Nsoh Fonchingong and Gemandze John Bobuin
Cameroon: The Stakes and Challenges of Governance and Development

Tatah Mentan
Democratizing or Reconfiguring Predatory Autocracy?
Myths and Realities in Africa Today

Roselyne M. Jua & Bate Besong
To the Budding Creative Writer: A Handbook

Albert Mukong
Prisonner without a Crime: Disciplining Dissent in Ahidjo's Cameroon

Mbuh Tennu Mbuh
In the Shadow of my Country

Bernard Nsokika Fonlon
Genuine Intellectuals: Academic and Social Responsibilities of Universities in Africa
Challenge of Culture in Africa: From Restoration to Integration

Lilian Lem Atanga
Gender, Discourse and Power in the Cameroonian Parliament

Cornelius Mbifung Lambi & Emmanuel Neba Ndenecho
Ecology and Natural Resource Development in the Western Highlands of Cameroon: Issues in Natural Resource Managment

Gideon F. For-mukwai
Facing Adversity with Audacity

Peter W. Vakunta & Bill F. Ndi
Nul n'a le monopole du français : deux poètes du Cameroon anglophone

Emmanuel Matateyou
Les murmures de l'harmattan

Ekpe Inyang
The Hill Barbers

JK Bannavti
Rock of God *(Kilán ke Nyiy)*

Godfrey B. Tangwa (Rotcod Gobata)
I Spit on their Graves: Testimony Relevant to the Democratization Struggle in Cameroon
Road Companion to Democracy and Meritocracy *(Further Essays from an African Perspective)*

Henrietta Mambo Nyamnjoh
"We Get Nothing from Fishishing", Fishing for Boat Opportunies amongst Senegalese Fisher Migrants

Bill F. Ndi, Dieurat Clervoyant & Peter W. Vakunta
Les douleurs de la plume noire : du Cameroun anglophone à Haïti

Laurence Juma
Kileleshwa: A Tale of Love, Betrayal and Corruption in Kenya

Nol Alembong
Forest Echoes (Poems)

Marie-Hélène Mottin-Sylla & Joëlle Palmieri
Excision : les jeunes changent l'Afrique par les TIC

Walter Gam Nkwi
Voicing the Voiceless: Contributions to Closing Gaps in Cameroon History, 1958-2009

John Koyela Fokwang
A Dictionary of Popular Bali Names

Alain-Joseph Sissao
(Translated from the French by Nina Tanti)
Folktales from the Moose of Burkina Faso

Colin Ayeab Diyen
The Earth in Peril

E. M. Chilver
Zintgraff's Explorations in Bamenda, Adamawa and the Benue Lands 1889—1892

Célestine Colette Fouellefak Kana
Valeurs religieuses et développement durable : une
approche d'analyse des institutions des Bamiléké du
Cameroun

Piet Konings
Crisis and Neoliberal Reforms in Africa: Civil Society and
Agro-Industry in Anglophone Cameroon's Plantation
Economy

Christopher Chi Che
Aspect of History, Language, Culture, Flora and Fauna

www.ingramcontent.com/pod-product-compliance
Lightning Source LLC
Chambersburg PA
CBHW020007290326
41935CB00007B/334